Drawing and Learning About Fish

Using Shapes and Lines

written and illustrated by
Amy Bailey Muehlenhardt

Thanks to our advisers for their expertise, research, and advice:

Linda Frichtel, Design Adjunct Faculty, MCAD
Minneapolis, Minnesota

Susan Kesselring, M.A., Literacy Educator
Rosemount–Apple Valley–Eagan (Minnesota) School District

PICTURE WINDOW BOOKS
Minneapolis, Minnesota

Amy Bailey Muehlenhardt grew up in Fergus Falls, Minnesota, and attended Minnesota State University in Moorhead. She holds a Bachelor of Science degree in Graphic Design and Art Education. Before coming to Picture Window Books, Amy was an elementary art teacher. She always impressed upon her students that "everyone is an artist." Amy lives in Mankato, Minnesota, with her husband, Brad, and daughter, Elise.

For Elise Lauren, my new smile.
ABM

Editorial Director: Carol Jones
Managing Editor: Catherine Neitge
Creative Director: Keith Griffin
Editor: Jill Kalz
Editorial Adviser: Bob Temple
Story Consultant: Terry Flaherty
Designer: Jaime Martens
Page Production: Picture Window Books
The illustrations in this book were created with pencil and colored pencil.

Picture Window Books
151 Good Counsel Drive
P.O. Box 669
Mankato, MN 56002-0669
1-877-845-8392
www.picturewindowbooks.com

Printed in the United States of America.

All books published by Picture Window Books are manufactured with paper containing at least 10 percent post-consumer waste.

Library of Congress Cataloging-in-Publication Data
Muehlenhardt, Amy Bailey, 1974–
Drawing and learning about fish / written and illustrated by Amy Bailey Muehlenhardt.
p. cm. — (Sketch it!)
Includes bibliographical references and index.
ISBN 978-1-4048-1192-8 (hardcover)
1. Fishes in art—Juvenile literature. 2. Drawing—Technique—Juvenile literature. I. Title: Fish. II. Title.
NC781.M84 2005
743.6'7—dc22   2005007174

Table of Contents

Everyone Is an Artist

There is no right or wrong way to draw!

With a little patience and some practice, anyone can learn to draw. Did you know every picture begins as a simple shape? If you can draw shapes, you can draw anything.

The Basics of Drawing

line—a long mark made by a pen, a pencil, or another tool

guideline—a line used to help you draw; the guideline will be erased when your drawing is almost complete

shade—to color in with your pencil

value—the lightness or darkness of an object

shape—the form or outline of an object or figure

diagonal—a shape or line that leans to the side

Before you begin, you will need

a pencil,
an eraser,
lots of paper!

Four Tips for Drawing

1. Draw very lightly.
Try drawing light, medium, and dark lines. The softer you press, the lighter the lines will be.

2. Draw your shapes.
When you are finished drawing, connect your shapes with a sketch line.

3. Add details.
Details are small things that make a good picture even better.

4. Color your art.
Use your colored pencils, crayons, or markers to create backgrounds.

Let's get started!

Simple shapes help you draw.

Practice drawing these shapes before you begin.

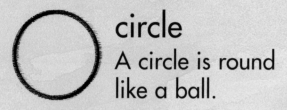 **circle**
A circle is round like a ball.

 **triangle**
A triangle has three sides and three corners.

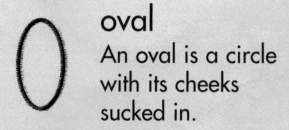 **oval**
An oval is a circle with its cheeks sucked in.

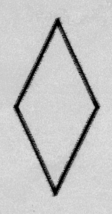 **diamond**
A diamond is two triangles put together.

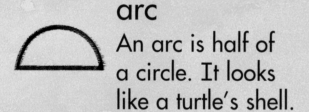 **arc**
An arc is half of a circle. It looks like a turtle's shell.

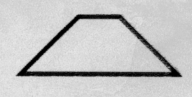 **trapezoid**
A trapezoid has four sides and four corners. Two of its sides are different lengths.

square
A square has four equal sides and four corners.

 **rectangle**
A rectangle has two long sides, two short sides, and four corners.

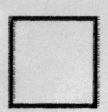 **crescent**
A crescent looks like a banana.

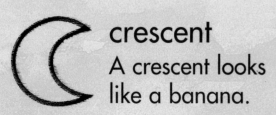

You will also use lines when drawing.

Practice drawing these lines.

vertical
A vertical line stands tall like a tree.

 **zigzag**
A zigzag line is sharp and pointy.

horizontal
A horizontal line lies down and takes a nap.

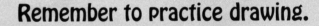 **wavy**
A wavy line moves up and down like a roller coaster.

diagonal
A diagonal line leans to the side.

Remember to practice drawing.

While using this book, you may want to stop drawing at step five or six. That's great! Everyone is at a different drawing level.

Don't worry if your picture isn't perfect. The important thing is to have fun.

 **dizzy**
A dizzy line spins around and around.

Be creative!

Alaskan King Salmon

Every fall, the Alaskan king salmon swims upstream to reach a calm place where it can lay its eggs. It's a difficult journey, as the fish often has to jump out of the water to pass over tiny waterfalls.

Step 1

Draw a large oval for the body. Add a small circle for the tail.

Step 2

Connect the oval to the circle with two horizontal lines. Overlap a trapezoid for the tail.

Step 3

Draw two triangles for the jaws. Draw a small circle inside the top triangle for the eye.

Step 4

Draw two triangles, two ovals, and an arc for the fins.

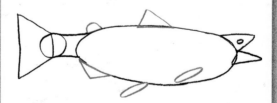

Step 5

Define the fish with a sketch line. When defining the tail, use a zigzag line.

Step 6

Erase the extra lines. Add details such as gills, scales, and a curved line on the salmon's side.

Step 7

Color your fish and add a background.

Blue Marlin

Blue on top and silver on the bottom, the blue marlin is a beautiful fish. It has long, pointed upper jaws that look like spears. It lives mostly in the Atlantic Ocean and can weigh up to 2,000 pounds (900 kilograms).

Step 1

Draw an oval for the body. Add two triangles for the upper and lower jaws.

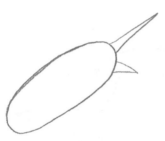

Step 2

Draw a small circle for the eye. Below the body draw a crescent for the tail.

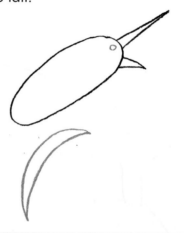

Step 3

Connect the body to the tail with two curved lines. Draw two curved lines for the fins.

Step 4

Draw two triangles for the bottom fins and a curved line for the large top fin.

Step 5

Finish the mouth with two zigzag lines. Define the fish with a sketch line.

Step 6

Erase the extra lines. Add details such as short lines on the top fin and a curved line along the marlin's side.

Step 7

Color your fish and add a background.

Guppy

The guppy is a pretty aquarium fish that makes a great pet. Its flashy tail and bright colors make it fun to watch. Female guppies give birth to tiny, live babies that start swimming right away.

Step 1

Draw two overlapping ovals for the body.

Step 2

Draw a triangle for the face. Add a small circle for the eye.

Step 3

Add a trapezoid for the tail.

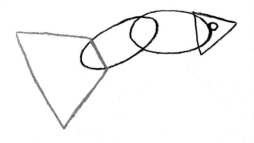

Step 4

Draw two zigzag lines for the fins.

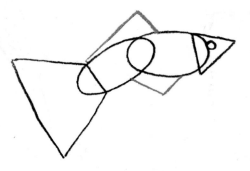

Step 5

Define the fish with a sketch line. Define the fins and tail with zigzag lines.

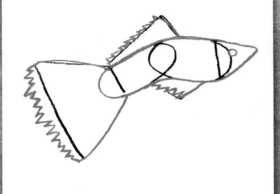

Step 6

Erase the extra lines. Add details such as gills, scales, and short lines on the fins and tail.

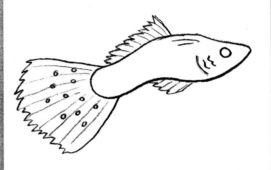

Step 7

Color your fish and add a background.

Bubble-Eye Goldfish

The bubble-eye goldfish makes a great pet because it's easy to care for. The bubble-eye is special because its eyes stick out from its head. They wobble around like big balloons as the goldfish swims.

Step 1

Draw an oval for the body. Draw two circles for the eyes. Add two dots for the pupils.

Step 2

Draw two large circles for the bubble eyes. The circles should overlap the fish.

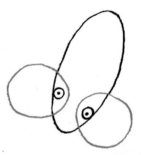

Step 3

Draw a curved line for the tail. Draw a diagonal line inside the tail.

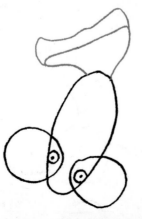

Step 4

Draw four ovals for the fins.

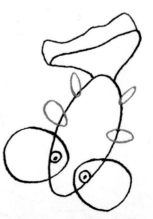

Step 5

Define the fish with a sketch line.

Step 6

Erase the extra lines. Connect the two bubble eyes with a curved line. Add details such as wavy lines for the scales.

Step 7

Color your fish and add a background.

Clownfish

The bright, colorful clownfish gets its name from its appearance—it looks like it's wearing an orange-and-white clown suit! In the ocean, clownfish lay their eggs on rocks protected by the tentacles of a sea anemone.

Step 1

Draw an oval for the body. Add a circle for the eye.

Step 2

Draw a circle for the tail.

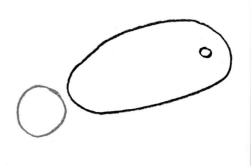

Step 3

Connect the body to the tail with two diagonal lines.

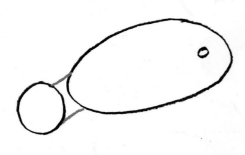

Step 4

Draw five curved lines for the fins.

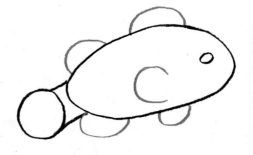

Step 5

Draw another curved line around each fin and the tail. Define the fish with a sketch line.

Step 6

Erase the extra lines. Add details such as curved lines for the stripes and a short line for the mouth.

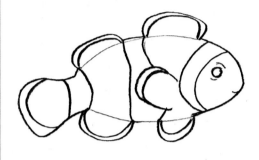

Step 7

Color your fish and add a background.

Angelfish

The black-striped angelfish is one of the most unique-looking aquarium fish. It seems to glide through the water without moving any fins, but its side fins push it along.

Step 1

Draw a trapezoid for the body. Add a small circle for the eye.

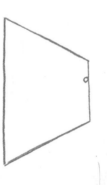

Step 2

Draw two arcs to complete the body.

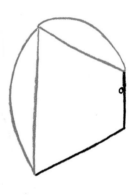

Step 3

Draw a rectangle and a trapezoid for the tail.

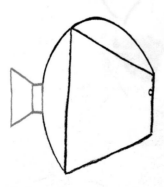

Step 4

Draw two ovals and two triangles for the fins. The top fin is a long, skinny triangle.

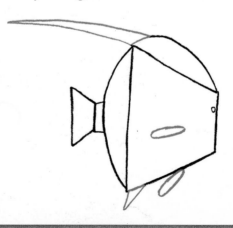

Step 5

Draw a curved line for the face. The angelfish has puckered lips. Define the fish with a sketch line.

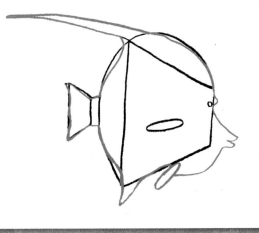

Step 6

Erase the extra lines. Add details such as curved lines for the stripes.

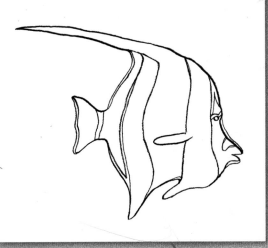

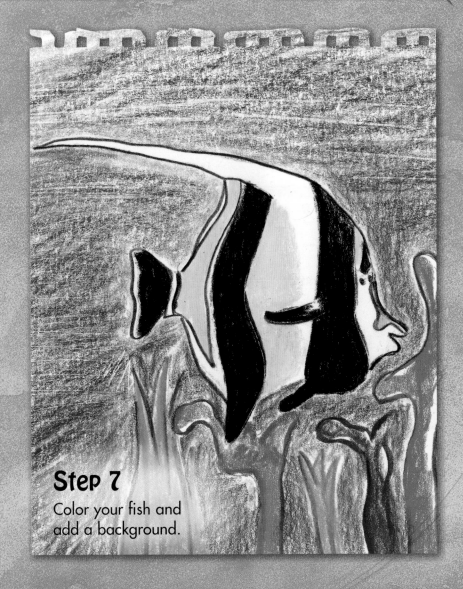

Step 7

Color your fish and add a background.

Humuhumu-nukunuku-a-pua'a

The state fish of Hawaii, the humuhumu-nukunuku-a-pua'a is also known as the reef triggerfish. Each of its eyes moves in a different direction, so the fish can look for food and watch for predators at the same time.

Step 1

Draw an oval for the body. Add a small circle for the tail.

Step 2

Draw two ovals for the eyes. Connect the tail to the body with two diagonal lines.

Step 3

Draw a trapezoid to complete the tail. Add an oval for the mouth.

Step 4

Draw two triangles and two arcs for the fins.

Step 5

Draw a curved line around the eye for the mask. Define the fish with a sketch line.

Step 6

Erase the extra lines. Add details such as lines on the tail and zigzag lines for the stripes.

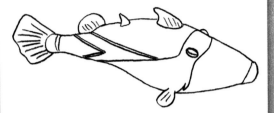

Step 7

Color your fish and add a background.

Largemouth Bass

The largemouth bass is a popular lake fish in the United States. It's usually green, with dark splotches that make a line down the side of its body. When it's hooked on a fishing line, it puts up a good fight.

Step 1

Draw an oval for the body. Add a small circle for the eye.

Step 2

Draw two circles and a triangle for the tail. Connect the body to the tail with two curved lines.

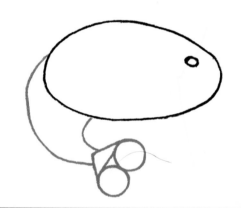

Step 3

Draw an arc and a triangle for the large mouth.

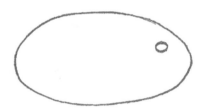

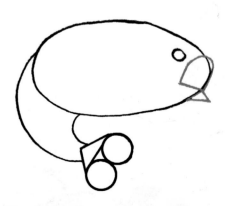

Step 4

Draw five curved lines for the fins. Add one tall arc for the side fin.

Step 5

Define the fish with a sketch line. The top fin has a curved sketch line. Add short lines to the top fin for the spines.

Step 6

Erase the extra lines. Add details such as curved lines for the gills.

Step 7

Color your fish and add a background.

To Learn More

At the Library

Levin, Freddie. *1-2-3 Draw Ocean Life: A Step-by-Step Guide*. Columbus, N.C.: Peel
    Productions, 2005.

Peterson, Tiffany. *Sea Creatures*. Chicago: Heinemann Library, 2003.

Soloff-Levy, Barbara. *How to Draw Aquarium Animals*. Mineola, N.Y.: Dover Publications,
    2003.

On the Web

FactHound offers a safe, fun way to find Web sites related to topics in this book.
All of the sites on FactHound have been researched by our staff.

1. Visit www.facthound.com
2. Type in this special code: 1404811923
3. Click on the FETCH IT button.

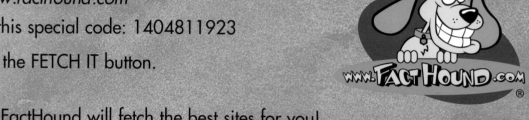

Your trusty FactHound will fetch the best sites for you!

Look for all the books in the Sketch It! series:
Drawing and Learning About ...

Bugs	Faces	Monsters
Cars	Fashion	Monster Trucks
Cats	Fish	
Dinosaurs	Horses	
Dogs	Jungle Animals